Satyress

Satyress

Audrey Molloy

SOUTHWORDeditions

First published in 2020
by Southword Editions
The Munster Literature Centre
Frank O'Connor House, 84 Douglas Street
Cork, Ireland

Set in Adobe Caslon 11.5pt

ISBN 978-1-905002-71-9

Contents

Acknowledgements

Grateful acknowledgement is made to the editors of the following publications in which these poems first appeared: *Cordite Poetry Review, F(r)iction, Headstuff, Magma Poetry, Meanjin, The North Magazine, Orbis Literary Journal, Popshot Magazine, Rabbit Poetry Journal, Rascal Journal, Shot Glass Journal* and *Southword*.

'Mother Creature' appeared in *Irises: The University of Canberra Vice-Chancellor's International Poetry Prize 2017*, edited by Monica Carroll and Paul Munden. 'On Reaching 45 the Poet Realises She Is Only 23' and 'Frisson' appeared in *NUI Galway ROPES Anthology 2018*, edited by Brendan Garrett. 'Symphony of Skin' appeared in *The Best New British and Irish Poets 2018* (Eyewear), edited by Maggie Smith. 'On Reaching 45 the Poet Realises She Is Only 23' and 'A Brief History of Smoking' appeared in *Aesthetica Creative Writing Annual 2020,* edited by Oz Hardwick. 'On Reaching 45 the Poet Realises She Is Only 23' appeared in *The Best New British and Irish Poets 2019-2020* (Eyewear), edited by Nick Makoha and Amira Ghanim.

Much gratitude is due to the following people, without whose encouragement, manuscript advice and friendship I would be lost: Jo Burns, Bobbie Sparrow, Ricky Ray, Barbara De Coursey Roy, Morag Anderson and all the other exceptionally kind and talented poets in my writing group, Poets Abroad; poet and mentor Anthony Lawrence, who has so generously shared his remarkable poetic insight; Kevin Higgins, who inspired many of these poems through his thoughtful prompts; Martina Evans, who selected my work for the Hennessy Emerging Poetry Award 2019; my early manuscript readers, including Maeve Valentine, Gary Valentine, Frances Browner and Geoff Callard, who provided priceless feedback on the emotional impact of the work; and my colleagues from the Poetry Ireland Introductions Series 2019. I am so grateful to have found my tribe.

I would not be a poet were it not for these people: my English teacher, Ita Cummings, who introduced me to many of the poets I still love today; my parents, Tom and Iris, who fostered my creativity; my children, Grace, Harry and Emily, who continue to startle me with their warmth and love; and my sweetheart, Graeme, whose presence in my life has made this book—and many other things—possible.

For B

ॐ

We call it *the body* but see only skin—
furred or bare—and a glimpse of pink whale
behind ivory teeth; a keratin sheet,
two holes to look in.

We call it an organ, as though it could play
melodies too low for ears—how else
could your skin call to mine
across oceans of husbands and wives?

ॐ

It happened quite by accident, snipping a loose thread from the hem of my corset, the blade nicked my thigh and the tiny wound ran round my leg tin-opener fashion. Not a drop of blood spilt, but my flesh rippled to the ground like a silk stocking freed from its garter on a close afternoon. Beneath, a taut and muscular thigh, covered in a gleaming coat of black hair. I was less shocked than you might imagine, thrilled, in fact, to make this discovery, so I set about freeing the rest of the leg. The ankle was a real sticking point and I had to sit on the floor, prising away flesh with a cheese knife, a box cutter for the tendons, tougher than steel, until there, on the parquetry, lay a coal-black neat and polished hoof. I was quicker with the second leg, applying lessons from the first. Already I could feel a surge of life through my veins, a snort in my nostrils. The gloves of my tired arms peeled away to new limbs of chestnut brown with willowy hands and fingernails like dogwood petals. Flaying the torso was painful, but how proud I was of my high round breasts, my belly rippling where it met the pelt reaching up to my waist. *You sexy fuck*, I whispered to the creature in my bathroom mirror, then grabbed each ear and pulled upwards. A lake of hair fell over my shoulder and down to my navel. My eyes were ringed with black paint, my mouth, cleft as a hare. This was no dream, I tell you; this was just the beginning. In my zeal I trod on my tail three times before draping it over my arm and, grabbing my best bag and throwing in the knives, I was off to where the wild ones go to dance among the boabs.

A Brief History of Smoking

i.

I blame Madonna. My fingerless gloves got me busted. Mother, always the *fashionista*, tried them on, held them to her cheek, blanched at the whiff of stale smoke and searched my room. The contraband, a pack of *Drum* (Mild Shag), was on my person as I followed her around, but she found it in the pocket of my blazer and burnt it in the Aga.

ii.

I'd dreamt of *Gauloises*, but that summer we smoked *Lucky Strikes*, lakeside in the Alps near Gap. We were tan, unaware of our taste in their mouths—the white-teeth boys who offered a light from brass Zippos. Delphine and I swam the lake to escape, walked back on virgin feet, laughing at nothing, bumming a smoke on the way, and who wouldn't give us one?

iii.

A pool of denim and velvet on the floor between bed and door; sending a taxi for smokes at 3 a.m.; all those things we don't do now, like cigarettes after sex—crackle as leaf becomes ash, sheets of smoke suspended, up-lit by a candle in a Mateus Rosé bottle. On the nightstand, like a carriage clock, *Dunhill*'s claret-and-gold pack; alas, now gone, replaced with images that would put you off coming.

iv.

Lighting up in the fire escape: me, filing clerk and hot CEO, who tells me I should wear red to work more often—you could back then. And the switch to *Silk Cut Ultra*, when you realise addiction is not strictly chemical. I mean how much nicotine is really in those things? Fourteen years post-quitting, the gaps—still there; after dessert, or making love, or when news comes on the phone that someone's died.

v.

The first time you have a panic attack you have no idea what's happening; only that you cannot read a simple instruction in English—how to call home from a public phone in an unfamiliar city; only nonsense words, and lungs that won't fill. Two good pulls on a *Rothmans* would've shit all over the Xanax they prescribed, but that only occurred to me years later.

vi.

They tell me I still have the smoker's personality, whatever that means: *extroverted, tense, impulsive, neurotic, sensation-seeking*— this last, I love: *the search for new, complex, intense experiences, and the predisposition to take risks in order to do so, including radical sports, criminal activities, risky sexual behavior, alcoholism, use of illicit drugs, gambling.* Well, maybe I have, and maybe I haven't.

vii.

And now we live to a hundred, nothing left to spare us from days spent lap-rugged in a wheelchair, staring through glass at pariahs huddled outside cafés and bars. (*Viva!* Vivienne Westwood, at the ball, pack of *Marlboro* tucked up the puff sleeve of her gown). Can it be that hard to create a smoke that might grant years of calm, and, one unexpected night, assassinate us in our sleep?

ENVY IS A DAYLILY

At the end of the street
behind the supermarket
where pretty houses peter out,
there's yours.

Broad-leaf weeds
outside the torn fly-screen,
where a Cavalier King Charles
eyes you, head to one side.

You can't answer his question,
but know this: someone
once looked upon your life
wishing it were theirs.

Mood Rings

There's a mood on the way to melancholia
right before the slide, the tinkle of light

piano in a minor key, how the sun's low angle
flatters your fickle hide,

how your face, reflected in a gallery window
looks momentarily like

Catherine Deneuve's—high cheekbones,
heavy eyelids shot in black and white.

You're glad you wore the fine black sweater
and your heirloom velvet jacket

though it doesn't suit the weather
and pearls are not in fashion

but neither is smoking, not even *Gauloises*,
not real cigarettes, just e-cigs

blowing mood rings for ambience
on a shelf above the abyss.

One note from an oboe and this moment's
the icing on the breeze-block in your pocket

and you know that in the likely event
of free-fall there's half a Valium in a locket

around your neck that you haven't needed so far
and that's reassuring; by now

you're so calm your chest barely rises, barely falls
and your aura turns aqua as you slide into blue.

STILL SEQUENCE: THE LAST YEAR

Jan

A man, one eyebrow raised, running fingertips around a dinner plate
for residue he cannot see because you should never trust a dishwasher.

Feb

A woman in a full-length white fur coat on a Moscow high street
pushing a child out of her path.

Mar

A rhino on the savannah standing downwind of a gunman, no scent
of threat; its great eyelashes sweep against its unseeing.

Apr

A mother in Sydney watching a film about a mother in Mumbai
sending lunch to the wrong husband.

May

A long letter in an inbox, read, unabsorbed, ignored.

Jun

An anniversary gift of a single ticket for a balloon ride at dawn
followed by champagne breakfast.

Jul

A dog, head cocked to decipher what's not said
by two people staring at the same screen.

Aug

A car parked in a driveway with Respighi's *The Birds* on repeat.

Sep

A carton of ice cream melting in a shopping trolley,
where a woman on a low wall talks on her phone.

Oct

A child freewheeling downhill with legs outstretched,
   finding her balance.

Nov

A park bench where a woman shares the same moon as her lover
   on the other side of the harbour.

Dec

A silver tree decoration on a fine, white ribbon, reflecting a family
   for one last time.

ELEGY FOR A LIMB

I'd forgotten how he takes his tea.
You'd think fourteen years with a man
would leave an imprint as detailed
as the fossil filaments of a feather;
the contours of his hands,
the half-moons of his fingernails.
Fingers are square, the jeweller said,
not round, if you look closely,
so he made a four-sided ring,
white gold with a dark sapphire.
The children said he lost it in the sea.

No milk, his hand blocks the cup.
Say hello to your mother from me, I want to say,
leaving your in-laws, almost as hard
as the rest of it—wounds that bleed for years,
amputations, missing fingers that still
twitch and drum, rub the edge of garments,
lost toes that tip you in their absence,
loosen your grip on things.

That Christmas after the split,
we spent the day together
as though nothing had happened;
their solemn faces on the screen after lunch,
Granny, older somehow; and the brother—
the gift of a brother in my family of sisters;
and the others, unable to smile
at the sight of the woman who left him,
even though, there I was, with the children
in their Kennedy clothes, and the carcass
of a bird on the dining table I would leave
that evening and not see again.

Where the Blue Flax Grows

Familiar now, as once the sheepskin boots
beneath the marriage bed,
this prairie is mine.

Thought I could walk out, given time,
didn't realise it was curved as a lie,
always leading back to centre.

I came here in mist, felt my way in.
My tinny voice echoes off its arcs,
like living in a washed-up whelk.

It opens up inside—a cliff over a beach.
I often walk here, trail biscotti crumbs
on the off chance I can find a way back.

Some days I hum a song:
La Marseillaise;
even *The Teddy-bear's Picnic*.

Once, I picked wildflowers until
I had a bucket full
of wilting yellow, blue and white.

It's good to keep occupied.

I can see the sharks from here—
their dark shapes slide back
and forth where my children wade.

I call out. Wind whips my vowels
          skyward
          until I'm empty of sound, a sealed jar.

The sharks whisper to each other,
sip their cappuccinos,
never blink.

He said he'd snuck out for the night, that he'd recently separated from the pre-frontal cortex of a doctor and what did I think of *that*? He wouldn't be drawn on the specialty, but it had to be an *ologist* of sorts—there was something of the teenager about his forearms, pale and smooth, his hands with their close-clipped fingernails that foretold microsurgery. While the doctor slept, tucked up next to his trophy wife, his ego had slipped from the house and that's how I found myself next to him at 4 a.m. in the garden bar. *You like my scrubs?* he asked with a flourish—cocky bastard—and all the while I was thinking they'd look better around his knees. But I said nothing and necked my tequila, licked the salt off the back of my hand, flicked my tail at a moth. It occurs to me now that my guilt was misplaced. I was on borrowed time myself; this would be no ordinary courtship. Reader, we needed no line of coke, no champagne fountain; it was going to happen and was simply a matter of where. A peacock screamed from the topiary. The best thing about a pelt, I discovered, as distinct from a frock or skinny jeans, is the freedom it affords shenanigans. This was hardly making love, but a savage mating among mock orange and fig. Damn him, he was good and he knew it; Navy-SEAL discipline and a few tricks up his pale-blue baggy sleeve. The stars had faded from the eastern sky by the time he anointed me, wiping his bristled chin across my high breasts, taut belly, furred thighs. A trickle of blood tattooed his shoulder. His lip was swollen where I'd silenced his bragging. We panted as pink dawn backlit the canopy. I didn't like it (my knees would ache for days) but who says it's supposed to be fun anyway? I kicked him off with my hooves and made my way back to the bar.

How to Love a Scribbly Gum

Study the creamy zigzagged skin
Decipher what others have failed to read
Trace the code with your fingertips
Catch its strains on the cockatoo's scream
Probe knotholes with your tongue
Smear the sap on your thighs and belly
Curl naked around the hollow trunk
Listen to the whisper of moth larvae
Reach up into the heartwood
Cradle it in your hands like truth

* The Scribbly Gum tree is endemic to the continent of Australia.

Seriously, Siri

At dawn the forest lies between me and my bed.
     I make my way home. Blackberries stain my mouth;
     I need sugar to stay alert but pelts have no pockets.
Politely, you say, *I'm not permitted to prepare food.*

I am foiled by your unswerving calm—
     a girl's got to lose her temper now and then.
  You wear patience like a lacy dress,
     seduce me with it,
     never raise your voice when I ignore directions.
Proceed to the route.

You'd make a great mother, I think,
     and wince at thoughts of my young, soon to wake.
     My memory, a jar of pickled experience;
       the small one standing by my bed—
       on her outstretched hand, a grain of sleep.
I can tell you where to find coffee.

My hooves are killing me!
  Surely best worn by four-legged beasts to spread the load.
     My coat is mud-caked to the knee. I need a bath.
     I cultivate your tone for domestic use:
I've found a number of plumbing suppliers. One is close to you.

The forest is a test: escape or find food—make your choice.
     I fossick for knobs of quartz to make a fire.
  Cloud shadows bruise the lake.
     I know where truffles stud the hazel,
     where the wood duck lays her eggs.
Beat until soft peaks form.

Now sun's up, bees *bitz* and *bitz*
  and you lead me to honey-combed morels
     near the crater's edge.

A pebble click-clacks to the lake.

Proceed to the route.
  Are you serious?
  I'm not allowed to be frivolous.

Mother Creature

Damselfly

Age thirteen, skin splits down her body.
She emerges, clad in shimmer, all sequin
and wing-glass. Pretty head thrown back, clasped
by mate after mate. Green river air: shantung
scribbled with their heart-shaped pen.

Salmon

Seaward, she's drawn tail-first. The river,
a silversmith, arming her, scale by scale.
The ocean has no boundary, save memory.
Though her flesh will coral with experience,
she'll dodge cane rod, vernal bear,
and return to the gravel of the smolt.

Pelican

Grotesque pink bill pressed to her quilled
leather corset releases the last minnow
from gular folds. If they want
to believe she pierces her bosom
to blood-nourish her young, let them.

Vixen

Bring on the night! Let her skulk
and cry, dog-fox by her side,
blackberry picking in fur coat and heels.
By dawn she's back to earth, her kits
an auburn ball. She'll carry the sick one
to the wood's edge and dump it. Just in case.

Pilot Whale

Her skin-rubber, hashed and scored
with scars, hides an armchair heart.
Her glands can still suckle a youngster
bored with waiting for his mother.
Her children's children will be doctors.

Frisson

i.

I plucked a fleck of lint
from your lapel in a polite sort of way
that day in the office.

How was I to know
it was the tip of a ribbon
as long as a river, red as a wound?

I pulled and pulled
until the room filled up—
a sea of scarlet bore us away.

ii.

In the false darkness of a bar at noon,
your eyes—a clearing in the woods,
where something catastrophic has struck

to let in light like that. I fear
you think I'm making this up,
all those tiny coincidences

like the photo of Al Pacino we notice
just after we talk of the movie, unaware
of the flame so close to our fuse.

I tell you Sting is even older than you
but the coin sticks and the jukebox
doesn't play and I know

this story may never unfold, only
in unspoken thoughts that emerge as moths,
phantoms imagined and glittering.

But you, old man, woken from torpor;
what made you grab this life
as she tried to slip from the room?

Double-Life Diary

Friday

6 p.m. Arsenic hour.
Nit combs, home-readers, sight-words,
permission-notes, show-and-tells.
Toilet-roll tubes and tape.
Sly-replies. Click-to-register.
She will coach their first season,
source satin ribbons in jewel colours
for girl-of-the-game, YouTube the rules.

Later. She will bleach the sink and pots.
Or write a poem. She will have the second
square of chocolate and a glass of Sancerre,
but abstain from all news and current affairs.
She will read *The Gift of Dyslexia* and weep,
or *The Captain's Verses* and sigh.
She'll dredge Barbie's vacant, smiling head
from a bath half-full of stagnant water.
Pilates tomorrow. Maybe.

Saturday

6 a.m. Her bed's a haven for brambled limbs
and fondant faces. *Quick, Mum, it's bin day.*
In her fug of sleep and lipstick they snuggle.
Pilates tomorrow, she vows.
She plumbs the washing basket,
constructing rogue-sock balls and tidy piles
of vests and knickers, like pancake stacks.

Noon. She bakes an orange cake,
halves the sugar, lets them break the eggs.
She'd knit them each a hat—nice for winter
or the glory box—but the ball of wool
unravels her, stitch by stitch,
then rolls on to undo someone else.

6 p.m. Drop-off time. She stocks the duffle bag
with yet more dovetailed socks, labeled shirts
and crisp pinafores for the black hole—
the one-way valve—Daddy's House.
Don't forget bunny. Big kiss for Mummy.

In the shower, she tries to scrub it off,
peel it from her body in long pink ribbons.
Your car, he says, *it doesn't smell like*
toast today, my love. She says,
I'll have to move the car before you ravish me,
my sweet. We are not paying for parking.

After the opera. A kiss against the wall
in the tomb-quiet, toy-strewn hall;
the squeak of Barbie's head under her bare heel,
the snap of Lego under his brogue.
Wait! she says, and stuffs on one more load
of socks so she can hang them out first thing.
Now they spoon in her new-sheeted bed,
the buzz of skin under fingertips,
the talk of Nabucco, Neruda, Nabokov.

Afterwards. She puzzles her reflection, cloven
by the make-up mirror: twelve selves
refracted from the bevel, yet she can live
only two lives, in a strange, marled existence.
Pilates tomorrow. Perhaps.

Sunday

6 a.m. Exhale. Float right leg to table-top.

The Landing

We were tossed, currach to sand,
each side of a line that once ran
like a guy-rope between us,
but now divided
          yours from mine, nothing
ours but a border.
I waited at the edge, looking for you.
When you returned you were older.
I was not.
          I probed my land learning
its secrets and now, when we love,
it is here on the edges of us, along
every twist and undulation—
          a line many times
                    longer than our mooring.

A Gradual Eden

After the lava had cooled,
hardened like a carapace
on the graves of our marriages,
nothing happened for a while.
Sure, you and I still talked all night,
once dared to walk arm-in-arm
like a real couple to the Vietnamese
restaurant with the string-bead curtain,
napkins folded into swans.
I had to learn the basics:
I only knew your thoughts,
but not, for instance, how you took
your coffee, how you swam at five
each day, leaving me to wake alone.
Nothing grew on the hard-baked
basalt of *us*. Ditches that defined
our lanes and highways vanished,
once-shady trees now jutted like antlers
where the lightning had struck them.
When the strawberries were gone
we ate dandelion and fiddle-head ferns.
You were an inventive chef, but I
was sick of roots and leaves; I wanted
Passiflora (or violets at the very least).
Once, longing for old comforts, you peeked
back under the edge of the rock-crust
for a glimpse of green, but the lawns
were mustard, thistle-pocked.
Twice I peeked too.
Watering didn't help much.
Neither did planting seeds.
After a year or two, we got used to it.
Gave up trying.
Hung up boots.
One day we saw the rock was dusted
with faintest green, just a bristle
like your beard at 5 a.m.—no more.
And then we saw a stem unfurl,
and then the flowers came.

The Tale of Lingchi

A happy housewife is all I wanted to be.
  To pack glass baubles in straw at Michaelmas,
    hum as I ironed shirts Sunday night,
  snip and file recipes,
  cut ham-and-cheese sandwiches into teddy-bear shapes.

I never signed up for knife-thrower's assistant.

 A man walks into a kitchen in his boxers
  in the small hours for a cup of warm milk
  because he cannot sleep.

Yet that's what I became: cool under fire,
  leather-buckled by wrist and ankle to oaken wheel,
  fixed smile turning up, turning down.

No one noticed the half-sadness, the blood
  that seeped from grazed breast or thigh,
  or spurted like a string of scarlet scarves
    pulled from a boy's ear.
  I was serene. Never sneezed.

 He smiles—must be sleepwalking—
  at the sight of the mud-caked form by the sink,
  jar of pickles in one hand, cheese knife in the other.

My skin loosened its hold, leaked quarter-
  formed notions as a torn net leaks minnows.
 I confided in no one—who'd believe me?
  The knife-thrower's woman wants for nothing,
  eats lobster mousseline in a velvet-lined boxcar
    when the crowds drift from the three-ring.

 But there's something of his wife's arse
  in the haunches of this she-beast gorging
  on Roquefort at the Carrara bench.

It was then I became anaemic;
    my heart startled up, pumped blood and notions
        faster round my limbs, filled my voice
        so it cried out with each hit
        (or miss, depending on your point of view).

The crowd squirmed and moved on to burlesque.
    But the tightrope walker caught my drift,
        with his supple feet and Jesus eyes.
                It was no affair. —A love story,
                the kind to bring down empires.

i.

It's been a while. The children, the divorce. Has it aged you? Your clear skin? Sydney is bright and shallow as a low-tide pool at *Plage des Cigales.* The harbour glitters like a rosary.

ii.

Those summers, *ma chérie!* Memory, clear as vermouth—tan limbs on a blue-hulled dinghy, six hands playing Satie on the piano in your room, the floor lamp draped in chiffon. And the way you wore them—no one wears scarves here, Delphine.

iii.

Red spatter of *coquelicots* in the fields—we didn't see them as omens. You were thinking about it, you said, and we laughed. I've heard you've lived variously since then, in drafty white houses, never far from the *tink tink* of halyards, lap of jetties, herring gulls' cries.

iv.

Admit it, Delphine; at fifteen a girl can love like a woman. Did you ever truly love him? That trip to Grenoble, you hovered near windows, green eyes fixed on the line where mackerel sky disappears and I knew. I forgave him. And you.

v.

They say you were taken by a shark, your mouth a perfect 'O', your mauves and pinks unraveled. I see you blood the waters where you stand, the smile widen on your thigh, the flash of sunlight off the bohemian blade, the crystal liquid percolate through bone, as you become the sea.

Ta fidèle amie

SYMPHONY OF SKIN

i.

They are there if you listen.
On the train, in the Laundromat—
the instruments, I mean;
bells, stirring in two-way
stretch cotton (their owner
slumped in the window seat,
his work boots tapping
a secret rhythm); timpani
buttoned under a cashier's blouse,
a cello bound by polyester pinafore
in salmon pink. She thinks
the air is flecked with soap dust,
doesn't realise it's rosin
from her bow. Air flows
through apertures where,
later, fingers will flutter,
strings blur under the rub
of horsehair; their discordant
mewl barely heard above
the swish of the train,
hum of machine, louder
in the darkness of tunnel
or the lull of rinse cycle,
then soft again. Tuning up,
they're getting ready
for this evening's symphony
of skin to begin
at precisely 10.15.

ii.

And you can never explain it
in physical terms—what happens
between two people
on an ordinary bed

in an ordinary room.
Let me ask, could you
school the cuttlefish
in Ludwig's *Emperor*
(second movement)
in terms of anvil, hammer
and stirrup? Paint the hues
of daybreak for the mole?
There is only air, compressed
and stretched. There is always
space between skins,
no matter how close they press.
No touch, only the music
of skin; an oboe sings,
a cello answers. .
Locked within the strands
of collagen, atoms built
of blocks, each one
a capsule packed with strings,
each string a note that's yet to play.

iii.

Afterwards, they lie curled,
two bass clefs facing this way,
that. They talk of anything,
of childhood; croak the lyrics
to Paul Simon songs,
this, the highlight, now
the players have left the stage.
Sleep will come later, a raft
pushed out on a starred sea.
What oak bed? Which room?
There is nothing here
but phosphorescence
along their border.
Only this small stage
drifting on the night swell,
a single baton on its floor.

ANNA KARENINA SMILES AS SHE STEPS OFF THE PLATFORM

Admit it, woman, to die not having lived is common.
    Who would trudge the poplar-lined avenue to where

it meets Moral High Ground? Who would not have gold
    fleck her eyes? Who wouldn't lunge into her bodice

to produce a shining meaty heart for all to look upon
    in curiosity? You chose to coat your daily bread

in butter, thick and yellow, chose *passiflora* over
    cabbage rose or chamomile. This path is narrow,

vine-choked, but runs true as the aorta. They say
    a woman only has so many heartbeats in her life

and yours are running low. You will have a sudden
    death—savage (yes!) as all best endings are, blood

returned to iron. Know you can hold your lovely head
    high in the station lamplight. Know you tried.

Notes

'A Brief History of Smoking' contains a quote from *Psychological characteristics associated with tobacco smoking behaviour* (Rondina et al, J. bras. pneumol. vol.33 no.5 São Paulo Sept./Oct. 2007).

'The Tale of Lingchi' was prompted by the opening line of Ocean Vuong's poem, 'Notebook Fragments.'

'Anna Karenina Smiles as She Steps off the Platform' was prompted by the opening line of Guy Goffette's poem, 'Letter to the Unknown Woman Across the Street III.'

Printed in Great Britain
by Amazon